This book belongs to

_____

Dedicated to my Papa and Everyone's Angels.

The Birthday of an Angel
Copyright © 2015 by Zoey Hess
All rights reserved.

ISBN 978-1-9415156-6-2
Library of Congress Control Number: 2015932602

Published by LongTale Publishing 6824 Long Drive Houston, Texas 77087.

Illustrations and Design by Ryan Shaw

First Edition
Printed in Canada

www.thebirthdayofanangel.com

The Birthday of an Angel

Written by Zoey Leslie Hess

Illustrated by Ryan Shaw

My grandpa passed away when I was six years old. Papa was one of the most important and special people in my life. He was more than just a grandpa. He was my everything.

$\mathcal{M}$y Papa was my best friend because he always came over to play games, read books, watch movies and draw with me. It didn't matter what we did, we always had a great time just being together.

The morning my Papa passed away, a beautiful, red cardinal sat on my kitchen window. From that day on, I saw cardinals everywhere, reminding me that Papa is my Angel and always watching over me.

That first year was pretty tough, and my life totally changed without him. I was so sad about losing someone so special to me.

I will never forget the night our family came together and my mom lit a candle. To my surprise, it had been a year since my Papa passed away.

In the Jewish religion, this is called a Yahrzeit [yahr-tsahyt] candle. The candle is lit every year to honor the day your loved one passed away.

The word Yahrzeit was hard for me to say and understand. So, I decided to say "Birthday of an Angel" instead to represent not my Papa dying but to celebrate the day he became an Angel.

I realized that even if Papa wasn't physically with me, there were other ways to know that he was still here. I saw and felt things in a more positive way by remembering all of our connections.

$\mathcal{M}$y Papa loved to give me gifts. My favorite gift from him was a stuffed Jiminy Cricket. Jiminy Cricket was a guardian to Pinocchio, just like Papa is to me. The stuffed animal still smells of my Papa's cologne and makes it seem as if he is here with me. You should never feel alone because there is always someone watching over you.

Papa and I loved collecting stamps together. I always thought the LOVE stamp collection was so pretty. Papa collected each one for me. One birthday he surprised me with a beautiful frame that had every LOVE stamp printed since the day I was born. What makes this gift even more special is on my ninth birthday, three years after my Papa passed away, I found a special card taped to the back of the frame he gave me. He wrote a very special message that I will always remember.

Dear Pretty Girl,

"Love...not time...heals all wounds."

Love,
Papa

When Papa was alive he loved to write and surprise me with notes and cards with very important messages and leave them all over the house. What a gift that even years after he passed away, he left me such a special card. This also shows me that Papa, as an Angel, is still sending me words of wisdom.

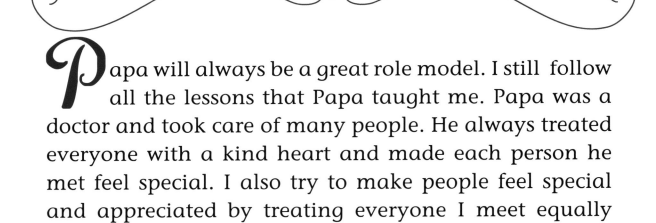

Papa will always be a great role model. I still follow all the lessons that Papa taught me. Papa was a doctor and took care of many people. He always treated everyone with a kind heart and made each person he met feel special. I also try to make people feel special and appreciated by treating everyone I meet equally with love, respect and kindness.

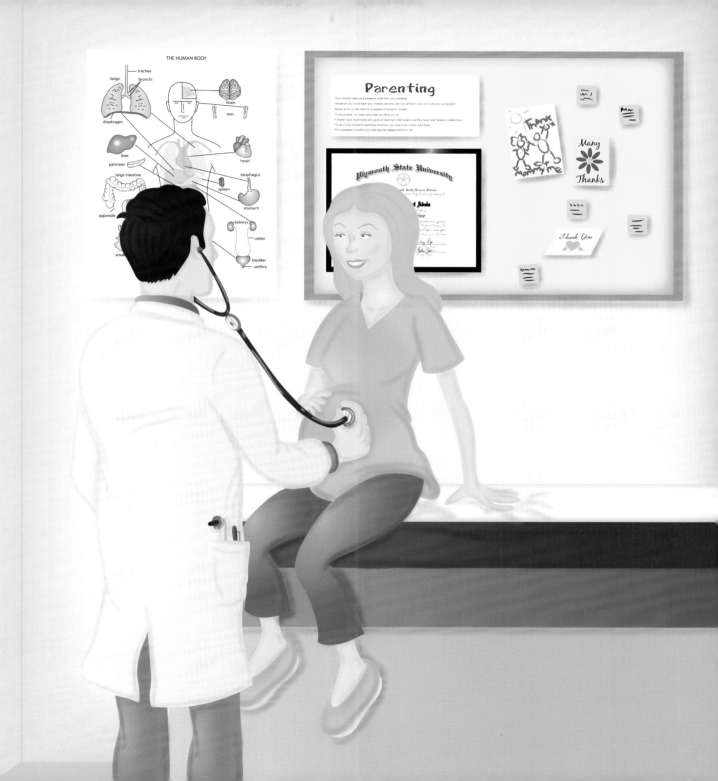

I think of my Papa every night before I go to bed. When Papa was alive, I used to call him before I would go to sleep, and we would say,

"Don't let the bed bugs bite … But if they do, hit them with your shoe. I LOVE YOU. Exclamation Mark!!!"

Now, I do this with my Mom and Dad. Saying this gives me a sense of comfort.

Before I go to sleep, I try to connect with Papa. I can hear
him, picture him and I feel him in my heart. One of the most
powerful messages he sent me was, "Heaven is a wonderful
and beautiful place, but don't rush your life to get there."
This helps me know that Papa is happy and where he needs
to be. I can see Papa sitting in his favorite big, blue chair
on top of white, fluffy clouds.

I want you to believe that love never dies. Your Angel will always be in your heart. Even if you can't touch them, there are always ways to feel them.

The next time you celebrate "The Birthday of an Angel," remember that your Angel is celebrating it with you.

About the Author

Zoey Leslie Hess is the Author of *The Birthday of an Angel*. Zoey is from Houston, Texas and is currently a 5th grader at Shlenker Elementary. Volleyball, tennis and art are her favorite activities.

Zoey lost her Papa in 2010 and wanted this book to explain how you can still have connections with your loved ones who have passed away.

Acknowledgements

I could not have made this book a reality without the help from my Mom & Dad, my sister Juliette, my publisher, Melissa Williams, and my illustrator, Ryan Shaw. Thank you for believing in me and making *The Birthday of an Angel* come alive.